How to Build a SKYSCRAPER

Contents

Written by Peter Gallivan

Collins

1 What is a skyscraper?

Across the world, cities are filling up with one type of building: the skyscraper. They are perfect examples of modern **engineering**, with huge glass windows, futuristic shapes and record-breaking heights.

Hong Kong harbour 2021

Skyscrapers are a special type of tall building. They are over 150 metres tall and have lots of space on each floor for people to live and work. They have only been around since the 1880s – before then, our cities looked very different.

Hong Kong harbour 1900

Humans have built tall buildings for thousands of years. We don't know why exactly, but historians think they were used for festivals, or to show off to others. Some of them are still standing, such as the pyramids in Egypt and Central America, but we only know about other tall buildings from historical writings.

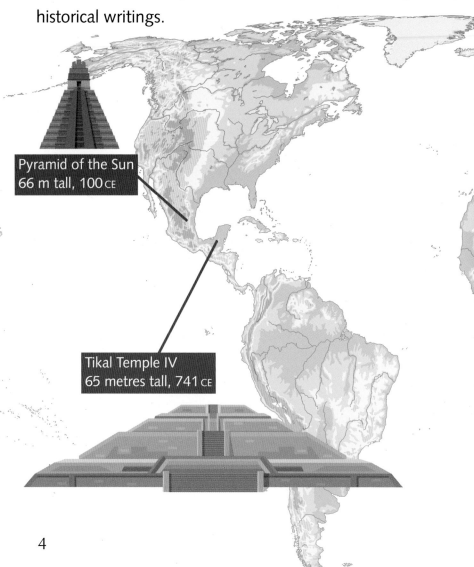

Pyramid of the Sun
66 m tall, 100 CE

Tikal Temple IV
65 metres tall, 741 CE

These early tall structures were not skyscrapers, because they did not have much space inside them – only a few small tunnels and chambers. They were mostly made of solid stone, built by stacking thousands of large blocks of stone on top of each other.

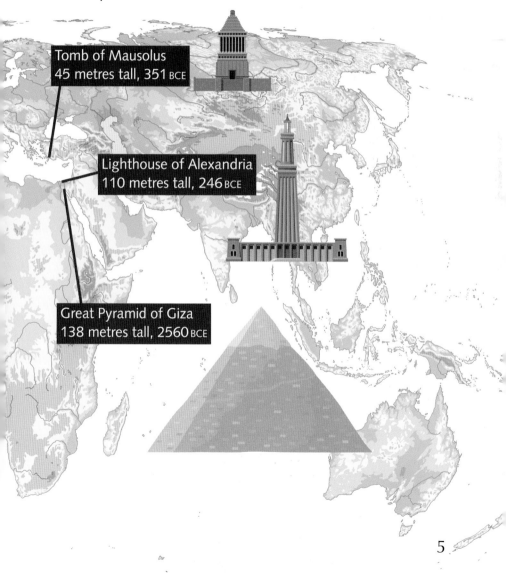

Tomb of Mausolus
45 metres tall, 351 BCE

Lighthouse of Alexandria
110 metres tall, 246 BCE

Great Pyramid of Giza
138 metres tall, 2560 BCE

The first skyscraper was the Home Insurance Building, started in 1884 in Chicago, USA. It wasn't built with stone but with new super-strong materials: **steel** and **concrete**. These materials helped make the building strong but used much less material. This meant the building had lots of floor space and was much higher than other buildings at the time.

an illustration of the Home Insurance Building being built (1885)

Home Insurance Building
55 metres, 12 floors (1926)

Soon, skyscrapers were being built around the world, getting taller each year. In 1931, the famous Empire State Building was built in New York, USA, which was the tallest in the world for 40 years. In the 1950s, skyscrapers started to use lots of glass, too. The UN Building in New York was the first with an all-glass **façade**, something seen on most skyscrapers today.

Empire State Building
381 metres, 102 floors (1931)

UN Building
154 metres, 39 floors (1948)

2 Who builds a skyscraper?

Building a skyscraper is a huge job, needing lots of people with different skills.

THE ARCHITECT

Job: plans and draws the overall design of the building.

Must: make sure a building has the right amount of space inside, but also that the outside looks good and fits in with its surroundings.

Did you know?

Architects sometimes design fantasy buildings to show what they think the future could be like. Frank Lloyd Wright was a famous American architect who designed a 4000-metre skyscraper called X-Seed 4000. If built, up to one million people could have lived inside!

THE STRUCTURAL ENGINEER

Job: turns the architect's plans into something which can be built.

Must: work out which materials to use and make sure the skyscraper will be safe and solid.

THE QUANTITY SURVEYOR

Job: decides what's needed to create the building.

Must: work out how much of the different building materials are needed and how many people are needed to build it.

THE TOWN PLANNER

Job: decides where a skyscraper can be built.

Must: make sure new skyscrapers fit alongside existing buildings and go with the overall plan for the city.

THE CONSTRUCTION WORKER

Job: the people who build the skyscraper.

Must: include specialist workers, such as people who work with steel, pour concrete or fit huge windows.

11

3 Where can skyscrapers be built?

Deciding where a skyscraper should be built is very important.

Across the world, cities are growing. This is why most skyscrapers are located in cities – they create more space for people to live in. This lets cities grow but still have space for parks and open spaces, so they don't feel overcrowded.

Hangzhou, China, a city of over 7 million people, has over 40 skyscrapers, but still lots of green space.

Sometimes skyscrapers are built where they aren't really needed. In Pyongyang, the capital city of North Korea, the unfinished Ryugyong Hotel stands. This is a record-breaking skyscraper for an unusual reason: it is the tallest **unoccupied** building in the world. The hotel was too large for the number of tourists visiting the city, and so it was never finished.

The Ryugyong Hotel is 330 metres tall with 105 floors.

When cities run out of space for new skyscrapers, they can now build new land in the sea. The small country of Singapore in Asia has added 141 square kilometres of new land since the 1960s – that's just under 20,000 football pitches! This area is filled with skyscrapers full of flats, hotels and shopping malls.

New land is built by dumping sand onto the seabed.

4 What are skyscrapers made from?

Skyscrapers are built with three main materials.

Concrete

An **artificial** alternative to stone, which can be made in any shape you need. When concrete is liquid it can be poured, but it becomes as hard and solid as rock when it dries out. Concrete was invented by the Romans – it is so strong that many Roman buildings still stand today, almost 2000 years later!

liquid concrete being poured

a wall of solid concrete

Steel

In the 1800s, scientists discovered that melting together iron and carbon made a new metal that was super-strong and **rigid**. They named it "steel". In buildings, steel is used as long beams which are lightweight, and help make large open spaces. It is also put inside concrete to make it even stronger.

liquid steel being poured

solid beams made of steel

Glass

Most modern skyscrapers have huge glass windows which let sunlight and warmth in, but keep rain and wind out. Glass is usually made of sand, heated to 1700°C. At this temperature, it becomes liquid, and can be poured into the shape of windows.

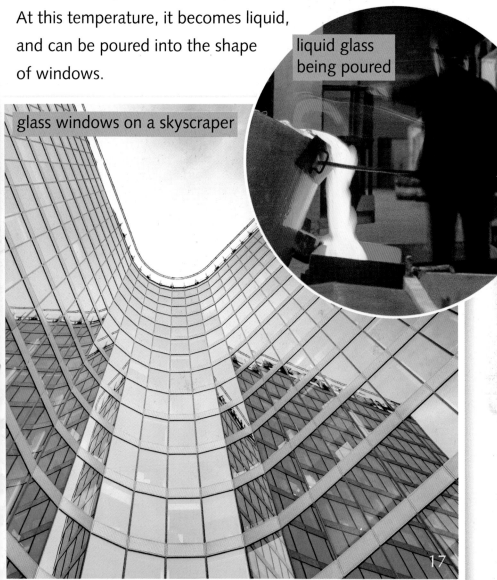

liquid glass being poured

glass windows on a skyscraper

Inside a skyscraper

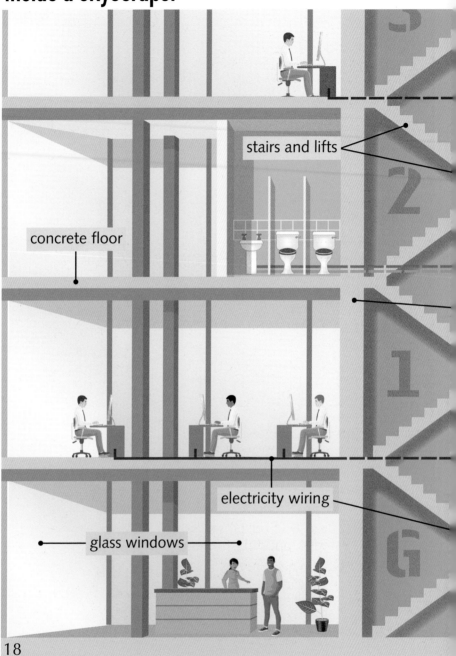

stairs and lifts

concrete floor

electricity wiring

glass windows

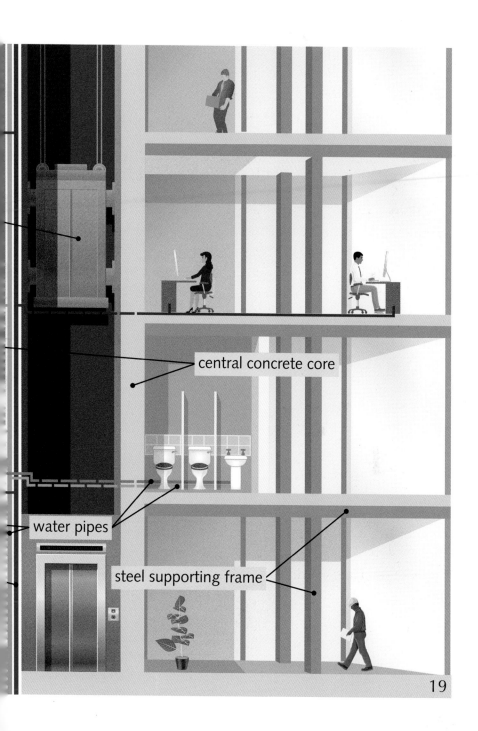

central concrete core

water pipes

steel supporting frame

19

5 How is a skyscraper built?

The foundations

The foundations are what fixes a skyscraper into
the ground, keeping it stable and upright like a tree's roots.
The ground beneath your feet is made from lots of
different layers, some of which are more solid than others.
Engineers test the ground first to see how solid it is before
deciding how deep to make the foundations.

construction workers
digging foundations
for a new skyscraper

Because they are so tall and heavy, skyscrapers have very deep foundations. The foundations for the Petronas Towers in Malaysia extend 120 metres underground – that's deeper than over 27 double-decker buses on top of each other! Skyscraper foundations are made of concrete and go through the softer soil into the more solid layers of **bedrock** underneath.

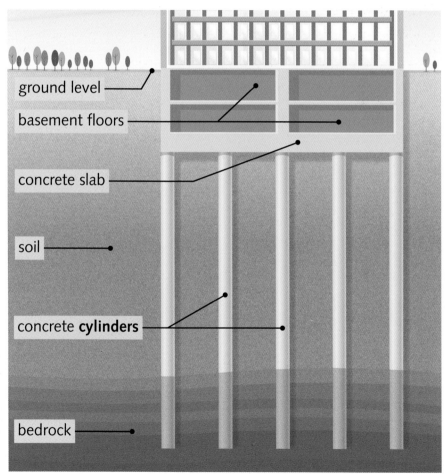

ground level

basement floors

concrete slab

soil

concrete **cylinders**

bedrock

Did you know?

Beneath Mexico City is an old lake, which has been slowly drained for drinking water, causing the ground to sink down. Because older building foundations were only built into this soft ground, the city is sinking – in some places by 30 centimetres a year! Today, skyscrapers in Mexico City are built with deep foundations, reaching the stable bedrock below the old lake.

It's very important to design foundations correctly – the Leaning Tower of Pisa in Italy shows what happens if not! It was built in 1173 CE from solid stone, which made it very heavy. Its foundations were much too shallow, and so it soon started sinking into the soft sandy soil, leaning over to one side.

The Leaning Tower of Pisa still leans today!

Floor by floor

Once the foundations are in place, a skyscraper is built floor by floor, rising up into the sky. All the materials are carried up by powerful cranes hundreds of metres above the city below.

A crane lifts a steel beam high above the city.

Did you know?

Modern cranes can carry up to 40 tonnes – the weight of about seven adult elephants! Cranes were first used for building by the ancient Greeks and Romans over 2,000 years ago. Their cranes were powered by people, but could lift up to 3 tonnes!

a model of a Roman crane

Riding to the top

Lifts are very important for quickly carrying people up hundreds of metres. The lift car is attached to a strong metal rope, which has a heavy weight on the other end. This means the rope can pull the car up and down. If the rope snaps, the lift has brakes to stop the car from falling.

Some lifts are on the outside of buildings, helping you see how they work.

Did you know?

The fastest lift in the world is in the CTF Finance Centre in Guangzhou, China. It travels up this 530-metre tower at an incredible 75 kilometres per hour. That's more than twice the top speed of most Olympic sprinters!

Guangzhou CTF Finance Centre

How high?

The 829-metre tall Burj Khalifa in Dubai has been the world's tallest skyscraper since 2009. But it might soon be beaten – the Jeddah Tower being built in Saudi Arabia is planned to be 1,000 metres tall. Dubai are planning the Dubai Creek Tower, which might have a gigantic height of 1,350 metres!

Dubai Creek Tower

It is very expensive to build super-tall skyscrapers, as they need bigger foundations and even more steel and concrete to support the weight of more floors above. This means that cities in the future will probably be filled with lots of medium-high skyscrapers, but not many as tall as the Burj Khalifa.

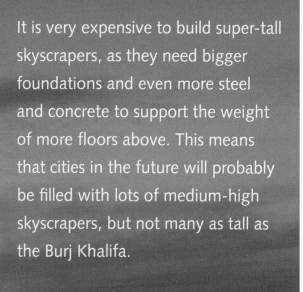

The Burj Khalifa is over ten years old but still dominates the Dubai skyline.

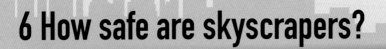

6 How safe are skyscrapers?

Windy wobbles

The wind gets stronger higher up from the ground, so is a big issue for super-tall skyscrapers, like the Burj Khalifa. This skyscraper has a special design, to help the wind to slip around it and not blow it over: it is not a **symmetrical** shape, it has rounded corners and is skinnier towards the top.

Burj Khalifa has 163 floors.

Skyscrapers are actually designed to sway in light winds. This stops them from getting damaged. If they didn't bend, light winds could crack and damage their steel frames.

Did you know?

The skinny 432 Park Avenue skyscraper in New York sways side to side by up to one metre.

432 Park Avenue is 426 metres high, with 85 floors.

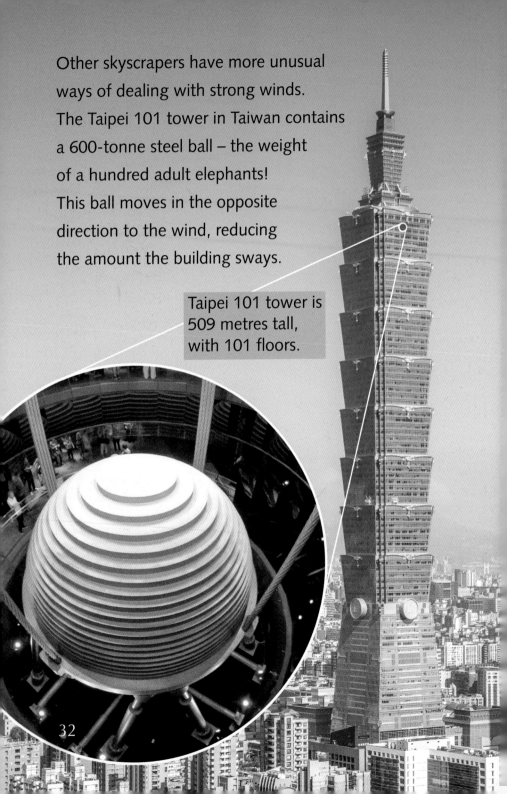

Other skyscrapers have more unusual ways of dealing with strong winds. The Taipei 101 tower in Taiwan contains a 600-tonne steel ball – the weight of a hundred adult elephants! This ball moves in the opposite direction to the wind, reducing the amount the building sways.

Taipei 101 tower is 509 metres tall, with 101 floors.

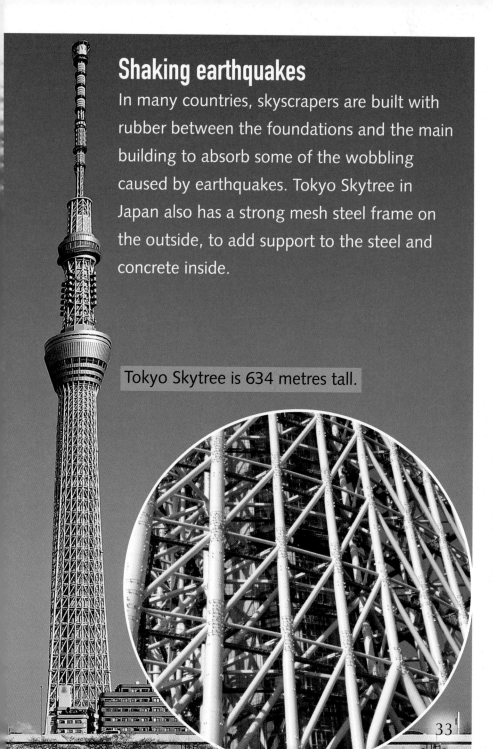

Shaking earthquakes

In many countries, skyscrapers are built with rubber between the foundations and the main building to absorb some of the wobbling caused by earthquakes. Tokyo Skytree in Japan also has a strong mesh steel frame on the outside, to add support to the steel and concrete inside.

Tokyo Skytree is 634 metres tall.

Stormy weather

Heavy rainfall can be a problem with skyscrapers too. Rainfall easily pours off their smooth sides, which might flood nearby areas. Covering the roof in soil and growing plants soaks up rainfall, which helps to reduce flooding and provides food and shelter for insects and birds.

You can see grasses and plants growing on these buildings – these are called green roofs.

In a storm, tall objects attract lightning, so most skyscrapers have a tall metal lightning rod on the roof, connected by wires down into the ground. This safely transfers a lightning strike into the earth, away from people.

lighting strikes the 546-metre tall One World Trade Center in New York City

Fire, fire!

Skyscrapers are too tall for a fire engine's hoses and ladders to reach the higher floors. Instead, skyscrapers are designed to stop a fire from spreading quickly, to give time for everyone to **evacuate** safely.

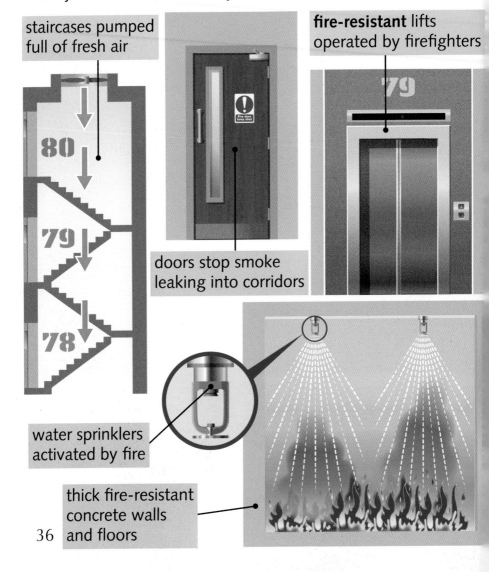

staircases pumped full of fresh air

fire-resistant lifts operated by firefighters

doors stop smoke leaking into corridors

water sprinklers activated by fire

thick fire-resistant concrete walls and floors

Engineers are testing new ideas for evacuating skyscrapers quickly!

parachutes

escape slides

zipwires

7 What might skyscrapers be like in the future?

Machine-made

Some smaller buildings are not built brick by brick, but by stacking together large pre-made sections. These sections are made in factories by giant robotic machines and contain everything, including windows and carpets. Building skyscrapers this way would be cheaper and much quicker.

a block of flats being built from pre-made sections

In 2018, a house was built in a completely new way: it was "printed" using a machine controlled by a computer. In the future, this technique could build a skyscraper without any humans.

To print a building, a machine squirts out layers of concrete, following a programmed plan. These layers build up to make walls just as strong as a normal house.

Looking after the environment

Concrete is not good for the environment – making it produces a lot of pollution and **greenhouse gases**, which cause **global warming**. Instead, engineers have started building skyscrapers with wood. It can be easily grown in forests and doesn't cause pollution, but needs clever design to make it work as well.

The 85-metre tall Mjøstårnet in Norway is the world's tallest wooden building.

Skyscrapers can also bring nature back.
In Milan, Italy, the Vertical Forest has been
built – two towers covered with 800 trees
and 20,000 plants. Filling our cities with
skyscrapers like these would help make our
cities greener, healthier and more beautiful
places to live in for everyone.

Here to stay

Humans have always built up towards the sky. The glass-covered giant skyscrapers that fill our cities today are great examples of what modern engineering can achieve. Across the globe there are now roughly 5000 skyscrapers, and more than 100 are built every year.

Skyscrapers help our cities to grow, making space for people to live, work and play. They may also help to save the planet, by transforming cities from grey spaces into plant-filled paradises. Whatever the cities of the future look like, skyscrapers will continue to be important features on our planet for a long time to come.

The cities of the future could be filled with skyscrapers while also being green and healthy.

Glossary

artificial something made by people and not found in nature

bedrock the solid layer of rock found underneath layers of soil

concrete a hard, rock-like material made by mixing sand, gravel, water and cement

cylinder a 3D form in the shape of a tube, with two flat, circular ends

engineering using maths and science to design and build things

evacuate to move out of a building to a place of safety

façade the front surface of a building

fire-resistant a material that can stop heat or fire

global warming the process of Earth warming up, caused by greenhouse gases trapping heat in the air

greenhouse gases gases released when fossil fuels (oil, natural gas and coal), solid waste, and wood products are burnt

rigid when something cannot easily be bent out of shape

steel a metal made by melting together iron and carbon at 1,600°C

symmetrical when a shape is the same on one side as the other

unoccupied when a building has no people inside it

Index

How to build a skyscraper

Where is there space to build?

Does a skyscraper fit into the plan for the city?

What will it be built from?

What will the skyscraper look like?

How tall will it be?

Is the land suitable for building on?

What weather will the skyscraper need to deal with?

What will happen in the skyscraper?

Will it be a hotel, or shops, or houses?

🐾 Ideas for reading 🐾

Written by Gill Matthews
Primary Literacy Consultant

Reading objectives:
- check that the text makes sense to them, discuss their understanding and explain the meaning of words in context
- retrieve and record information from non-fiction
- ask questions to improve their understanding of a text

Spoken language objectives:
- use spoken language to develop understanding through speculating, hypothesising, imagining and exploring ideas
- participate in discussions, presentations, performances, role play, improvisations and debates

Curriculum links: Design and Technology

Interest words: transforming, paradises, features

Resources: Model making materials, IT

Build a context for reading

- Ask children to look at the front cover and to read the title. Explore what children know about skyscrapers.
- Read the back-cover blurb. Ask children to suggest how skyscrapers might be built and what they might be made of.
- Discuss what kind of book this is. Ask what kind of features it might have. Give children time to skim the book to find the contents, glossary and index. Discuss the purpose of these features and how they are organised. Give children the opportunity to use the contents and index to look up information.

Understand and apply reading strategies

- Read pp2–7 aloud. Ask children why they think the word *engineering* (p2) is in bold. Give them time to look up the entry in the glossary.
- Ask children to compare the two images on pp2–3. Discuss the differences they can see.